# Ancient Achievements

Instructor's Handbook

A Demme Learning Publication

**Ancient Achievements Instructor's Handbook**
©2014 Spelling You See
©2013 Karen J. Holinga, PhD.
Published and distributed by Demme Learning

www.SpellingYouSee.com

1-888-854-6284 or +1 717-283-1448 | www.demmelearning.com
Lancaster, Pennsylvania USA

ISBN 978-1-60826-620-3
Revision Code 1014

Printed in the United States of America by Bindery Associates LLC

For information regarding CPSIA on this printed material call: 1-888-854-6284 and provide reference #0616-07272016

# Meet Demme Learning

Demme Learning has been providing innovative learning solutions for homeschoolers, parents, and small group learning environments since 1990. Based in Lancaster, Pennsylvania, Demme Learning is an independent family-owned and operated publishing company.

The Demme Learning family of products are designed around the involvement of an engaged parent. We recognize that engaged parents are crucial to children's success in becoming lifelong learners. Engaged parents may be primary or supplemental instructors in their child's education. Each of our products also builds on these principles: multi-sensory instruction; sequential instruction that builds from concept to concept to achieve mastery; guided discovery; and individualized instruction that adapts to each student's unique strengths.

**Visit *demmelearning.com* to learn more about us and our philosophy of education.**

## Meet our family of products

### Math-U-See is Math You'll Love.

Math-U-See is a complete K–12 math curriculum that uses manipulatives to illustrate and teach math concepts. We "Build Understanding" in students with a multi-sensory, mastery-based approach suitable for all levels and learning styles. **Visit *mathusee.com* to learn more.**

### A Unique Approach to Learning Spelling

Our program allows students to develop skills naturally, at their own pace, with the instructor's direction and encouragement. Colorful, interesting reading passages at an appropriate developmental level allow students to learn words in context, committing spelling to long-term memory. **Visit *spellingyousee.com* to learn more.**

### A Parents' Guide to the Best Educational Apps for Kids

KinderTown turns your device into an educational playground with apps reviewed by childhood educators. We show only the best apps, organized by subject to easily find just what you're looking for. **Visit *kindertown.com* to learn more about our review process or to download the free app.**

### The Family That Stays Together, Stays Together.

The family ministry of Steve Demme; with lectures, seminars, and books, Building Faith Families endeavors to support the key component of building lifelong learners—the engaged parent. **Visit *buildingfaithfamilies.org* to learn more.**

## About Spelling You See

This innovative approach to spelling was developed by Dr. Karen Holinga, a former teacher and college professor with over 30 years of experience working with children. A qualified reading specialist, Dr. Holinga has operated a busy clinic in Ohio since 2000, helping hundreds of children become confident, successful spellers. The design of this program allows students to develop spelling skills naturally, at their own pace, supported by the direction and encouragement of the instructor.

There are no weekly spelling lists or spelling tests and no time-consuming instructor preparation. Instead, brief daily activities help students integrate writing, reading, speaking, and listening. As a result, they develop a long-term visual memory for everyday words. This prepares students for more detailed study of word patterns as they move to the advanced stages of spelling.

Visit *spellingyousee.com* for more information about Dr. Karen Holinga and Spelling You See.

# Introduction

# About *Ancient Achievements*

## Weekly Activity Guide

# Resources

# Philosophy

*"Those who set out to remember every letter of every word will never make it. Those who try to spell by sound alone will be defeated. Those who learn how to 'walk through' words with sensible expectations, noting sound, pattern, and meaning relationships, will know what to remember, and they will learn to spell English."*

–EDMUND HENDERSON, 1990, p. 70

Teaching spelling can be difficult and frustrating. No matter how hard we work, and regardless of how many rules we learn, we always encounter exceptions. They are inevitable because the English language has evolved from so many different languages. We cannot consistently predict which pattern or rule will apply.

Most spelling programs are based on the premise that if children memorize a certain sequence of letters or words, they will become good spellers. The procedure is to present a word list to the children on Monday, have them study it in various ways all week, take the test on Friday, and expect them to spell each word correctly the next time they write. This approach does not work well because the brain perceives these word lists as item knowledge. Without something meaningful to connect the words to—without linkage— the brain simply reverts to rote memory, storing the words for a few days and then discarding them. The words never make it into long-term memory.

Decades ago a linguist named Charles Read (1971) noticed that preschoolers made consistent and similar assumptions about words when they were trying to figure out how to spell. From that landmark observation, numerous other researchers from the University of Virginia, headed by Edmund Henderson, confirmed and extended Read's work.

Their various studies suggested that spellers advance through a common progression, starting with sound-to-letter correspondence and moving toward more advanced and complicated spelling structures. Eventually, after years of observations and study, this group of university professors presented a model of developmental spelling based on the consistent, sequential stages through which all students move.

The developmental process of spelling is similar to what children go through when learning to walk. They need to develop the prerequisite skill of crawling before they can move on to walking and then running. In the same way, this program guides your student naturally through the stages in the process of learning to spell.

## The Five Developmental Stages of Spelling

All students move through these five stages as they learn to spell:

Stage I: Preliterate

Stage II: Phonetic

Stage III: Skill Development

Stage IV: Word Extension

Stage V: Derivational Constancy

### Stage I: Preliterate

Before children can read, write, or spell, they must first acquire some fundamental understandings about language. This process occurs during the preliterate stage. As children experience the printed page, both as a result of watching books being read and of exploring books on their own, they develop concepts of print. For example, they become aware that English words are written from left to right and flow from the top to the bottom of the page. Beginning writing experiences might include "pretend writing" with scribbles or random marks that eventually become more linear. Children then learn to write actual letters, often beginning with their own names, showing words as strings of letters or letter-like symbols. These activities lay the foundation for the language skills that are developed in the next stage.

### Stage II: Phonetic

The second developmental stage is auditory. As children are increasingly exposed to language, they develop phonemic awareness—the ability to distinguish the individual sounds that make up spoken words in English. They then relate these sounds to print by understanding that letters represent sounds, letters make up words, and that each word looks different.

In the phonetic stage, most instruction involves helping children match individual sounds in words to their corresponding letters, usually starting with their own names. They often use all capital letters and spell words incorrectly. For example, they may spell *KAT* for *cat*, *MI* for *my*, *LUV* for *love*, and *U* for *you*. Silent letters in words like *bake* or *lamb* may be omitted. Instructors welcome these spellings as an indication that the student is beginning to understand sound-to-letter correspondence. Children arrive at the end of the phonetic stage once they have learned the basic rules of phonics and can actively apply them to both reading and spelling.

## Stage III: Skill Development

This third developmental stage is the most difficult, the most critical, and the longest for emerging spellers. It usually begins once children have cracked the basic phonetic code and are progressing rapidly in reading. As students learn the phonics rules needed to develop reading skill, they are able to apply these rules to their spelling. Problems often arise, however, when children become aware of words that are not spelled phonetically, such as *house*, *there*, and *said*. Phonics rules need to be de-emphasized at this stage because they are no longer needed to help the student learn to read. In fact, over-teaching phonics at this stage can actually create unnecessary confusion in spelling. The overriding neurological principle is that, because of the numerous inconsistencies in our language, new and different spellings must be connected to context in order for the new information to be linked correctly and permanently to long-term memory. As students encounter new vocabulary over several grade levels, spelling skill increases as they apply consistent strategies to master more complex spelling patterns and a greater number of irregularly-spelled words.

The critical thing to remember is that this is a stage—a developmental link to the stages that follow. Children are often in the skill-development stage through the fifth grade or later. It may seem repetitious to practice the same skills over and over again, year after year. However, if students do not master these skills, it is very difficult for them to move ahead in spelling development.

## Stage IV: Word Extension

A much more complicated stage—the word-extension stage—focuses on syllables within words, as well as prefixes and suffixes. In the upper elementary or intermediate grades, children often struggle with issues such as doubling consonants when changing the endings (*pot/potting,* but *look/looking*) and dropping the final *e* before adding an ending (*love/loving,* but *excite/excitement*). Other issues arise with words such as *almost*. Why isn't it spelled *allmost*? Often the brightest children become the most confused or exasperated by these inconsistencies, but they eventually learn to master them as they move through this stage of development.

## Stage V: Derivational Constancy

This final stage explores related words—those with the same derivation or origin— that usually have a consistent pattern despite changes in pronunciation. These words are often predictable if a student is familiar with word roots. Greek and Latin root study is helpful at this stage as mature spellers gain an understanding of how patterns and meaning are related. Students gain the most benefit from this stage if they begin derivational studies after basic vocabulary has been learned and a strong foundation has been built in the previous stages.

It is important to note that children must move through these developmental stages sequentially. Each stage builds on the previous one. Because they are developmental in nature, stages in spelling do not necessarily correspond to reading levels. In order to become a good speller in English, one must develop a strong visual memory, and for young children this can be very difficult. Even if a child excels in reading, spelling can lag far behind. It is essential that parents and teachers understand the developmental nature of the spelling process in order to guide the child effectively through the different stages.

# Curriculum Sequence and Placement Guidelines

| Level | Title |
|---|---|
| Level A | *Listen and Write* |
| Level B | *Jack and Jill* |
| Level C | *Wild Tales* |
| Level D | *Americana* |
| Level E | *American Spirit* |
| Level F | *Ancient Achievements* |
| Level G | *Modern Milestones* |

- Do not try to match the student's reading level to an equivalent spelling level. Students must master each developmental stage of spelling before advancing to the next. Research has not established a correlation between reading achievement and spelling ability. No one can "skip" stages in spelling.

- *Listen and Write* is for a beginning reader who is learning letter names and sounds and how to hold a pencil properly when writing.

- *Jack and Jill* is for a student who prints easily with lowercase letters and knows most sounds, including long and short vowels.

- *Wild Tales* is for a student who knows all letter sounds, spells many common words correctly, and is becoming comfortable with reading.

- *Americana* is for a proficient reader with gradually-improving spelling skills.

- *American Spirit* is for a student who is able to spell many common words confidently but may not be ready for the more advanced content of the next level.

- *Ancient Achievements* is for a student who is nearing the end of the Skill Development stage. It provides skill review and an introduction to the next two stages of spelling.

- *Modern Milestones* is for a student who is ready for the Word Extension stage of spelling. The student should be able to follow written directions and work independently.

- You can find detailed skill assessments for each level at spellingyousee.com.

# About Ancient Achievements

## Getting Started

### Overview

*Ancient Achievements* features stories from faraway times and places. Topics include ancient writing systems, the production of silk, mountainside terraces in the Philippines, the English longbow, Viking ships, and Incan counting systems. Students will read and study a different passage each week.

### Stepping Up

A student using *Ancient Achievements* should be comfortable spelling many everyday words. However, his growing vocabulary will add to the number of words that he needs to be able to spell confidently. For this reason, students using *Ancient Achievements* are still primarily in the Skill Development stage of spelling. At the same time, students are becoming increasingly aware of patterns within words and relationships between words. In addition to the familiar core activities of chunking, copywork, and dictation, each lesson in *Ancient Achievements* includes a Spotlight which provides interesting facts about words and the relationships between them. The goal is to stimulate curiosity about words and to prepare students for Word Extension, the stage of spelling that will be addressed in *Modern Milestones*.

### Needed Items

To complete the daily lessons, your student will need a regular pencil and colored pencils or highlighters (blue, green, yellow, pink or red, purple, and orange).

### The Core Activities

This spelling program includes three core student activities that will be familiar to students who have previously used Spelling You See: chunking, copywork, and dictation. These activities are not randomly selected to fill time and pages; each is important in helping the brain learn spelling patterns.

Chunking each passage provides hands-on experience with the many irregular letter patterns in English. Copywork and dictation require the brain to pay attention to details in the print within a meaningful context. Together, these three activities move words into the long-term memory and produce students who are competent spellers.

## Daily Worksheets

Each of the 36 weekly lessons is divided into five parts, A through E. In the *Student Workbook*, a day's activity consists of two facing pages. Each day, the student reads the passage aloud to the instructor, with the instructor helping with the pronunciation of any unfamiliar words. The next step is for the student to find and mark various letter patterns in the passage in a process called *chunking*. Students will also have opportunities throughout the week for copywork and writing from dictation.

## Spotlights

Each lesson in *Ancient Achievements* features a Spotlight that calls attention to one or more of the words in the passage. The purpose is to stimulate curiosity about words and to prepare students for future skill levels of spelling. The instructions in the *Handbook* offer ideas for further activities involving the spotlighted words. Let your student's interest determine how much time is spent on these optional activities.

## Tips for Success

This *Handbook* gives lesson-by-lesson instructions for *Ancient Achievements*. Answers for questions asked in the Spotlights are included in the instructions for each lesson. The lesson instructions may also include more information about the passage or suggestions for optional activities. There is detailed information about chunking, copywork, and dictation beginning on page 33. Use the **Glossary** that begins on page 64 to clarify the meaning of any unfamiliar terms.

Keep the lessons short and upbeat. Although students using this level may be able to work fairly independently, do not hesitate to offer as much help as is needed to ensure success.

The **Answer Key** begins on page 50 of this *Instructor's Handbook*.

## Online Resources for This Level

Each level has an online page with links to additional materials and resources to enhance your instructional program. If you need help accessing your online resources, please contact a Customer Service Representative.

# Lesson-by-Lesson Instructions

## Lesson 1: Cave of Lascaux (Vowel Chunks)

- Lesson 1 introduces vowel chunks. The vowels are *a, e, i, o, u,* and sometimes *y* and *w*; a vowel chunk is a combination of vowels that usually makes one sound, such as *ea, oo,* and *ou*. Focusing on letter patterns in a meaningful context helps a student learn the irregular sounds of the English language.

- On Day 1, have the student read the passage aloud, offering help with pronunciation if needed. (The word *Lascaux* is pronounced *la-SKO*.) Then have her use a yellow pencil or highlighter to mark the vowel chunks. As you move through *Ancient Achievements*, each letter pattern will be assigned its own color. Using the colors consistently will help your student visually learn the spelling patterns. Use the color-coded **Answer Key** in the back of this *Handbook* to make sure the chunking is complete on each page. If necessary, point out any vowel chunks that were overlooked and have your student mark them. This chunking activity will be repeated on each day of the lesson.

- Have the student copy as much of the passage on the right-hand page as he can complete in 10 minutes. Have him mark the vowel chunks on his written copy, using the left-hand page for a guide as needed.

- On Days 2 and 3, repeat the reading, chunking, and copywork as you did on Day 1 of the lesson.

- On Day 3, the Spotlight encourages students to look for rhyming words. It can be helpful to associate words that have similar letter patterns. Marking the patterns repeatedly throughout this course will help your student make these associations; however, be sure your student understands that not all words that rhyme have the same letter pattern.

- Some other words that rhyme with *paint* and have the *ai* vowel chunk are *saint, complaint,* and *quaint*. If you wish, have your student write each of these words and discuss their meanings. You and your student may want to make up sentences using each word.

- On Day 4, you will dictate the passage for your student to write. In the **Resources** section in the back of this *Handbook*, you will find a copy of the passage that you can use for dictation. When you are ready to begin, place a sheet of paper over the passage on the left-hand page in the student book and read the passage from the *Handbook*. Encourage the student to relax and let her know that you will offer as much help as is needed. Remember that the dictation exercise is not a test. Go as slowly as is needed for the student to write without confusion or frustration. Offer help as soon as a word is misspelled. After 10 minutes, stop the dictation and count the number of words written correctly. Record that number at the bottom of the student page. You can read more important information about dictation on page 36.

- On Day 5, the student will have a second opportunity to write the passage from dictation. This dictation is a little different, as you will not help the student spell any words. Instead, challenge him to try difficult words until they look right. You may cover the printed passage with a sheet of paper and use the passage from the back of this book for dictation. Continue to limit the time spent on dictation to 10 minutes. You may provide correct punctuation and capitalization. Count and record the number of words spelled correctly, but remember that this is not a test. If the first dictation was completed easily, you may want to skip this second dictation.

## Lesson 2: Goseck Circle (Vowel Chunks)

- In Lesson 2, your student will continue to focus on vowel chunks. Have your student mark the chunks in the passage and in the copywork each day.

- When completing copywork, your student should feel free to erase mistakes and rewrite the word. It is important that he practice writing words correctly rather than incorrectly.

- Note that many sources prefer the spelling *archaeology* to *archeology*, but both are considered correct.

- Challenge your student to identify other words that end in *-ology*. Some examples are *technology*, *psychology*, *mythology*, and *theology*.

## Lesson 3: Cuneiform (Consonant Chunks)

- Lesson 3 introduces consonant chunks. The consonants are all the letters that are not vowels. A consonant chunk is comprised of two consonants that usually make one sound in a word, such as *th* or *kn*. Double consonants that make one sound are also considered consonant chunks. A complete list of consonant chunks can be found on page 34. They should be marked in blue.

- Point out to your student that, while some of the letters in the consonant chunks make the sounds that you might expect, others are silent, and some letters change their sounds completely when they appear in a chunk.

- Blends are not included with the consonant chunks. In a blend, each letter can be heard making its expected sound. The *st* in *stop* is an example of a blend.

- The Spotlight for this lesson introduces another context where the word *cuneiform* is used. Point out that the English language was developed from several other languages. This has resulted in a very rich language with many interesting words, but it has also resulted in many seemingly-inconsistent spellings. Many of these spellings are actually clues about the history of words.

- When your student is writing from dictation, she should not stop to erase a word that she thinks is incorrect. Instead, she should simply cross out the incorrect word and write it again. Be sure to offer as much help as is needed for the first dictation exercise of each week.

- If all five parts of a lesson have not been completed by the end of a week, feel free to begin a new lesson the following week. Common words and letter patterns will be repeated many times throughout the course. It is more important that a student feel that he is successfully making progress than to ensure that every page is completed.

## Lesson 4: Chinese Silk (Consonant Chunks)

- In Lesson 4, your student will continue to focus on consonant chunks. Be sure to have your student read the passage aloud to you each day.

- The Spotlight for this lesson calls attention to the *cent* in *centuries*. Some other interesting time words with Latin roots are *decade* (10 years) and *millennium* (1000 years).

## Lesson 5: Mummies (Vowel and Consonant Chunks)

- This lesson requires the student to mark or "chunk" both vowel and consonant groups. This may be challenging at first, so work carefully with your student. After chunking the first page of each lesson, compare the student's work to the **Answer Key** in the back of this *Handbook*. Then the student can use the first page of the lesson to check his work throughout the week. Remember that chunking is a learning tool, not a test.

- The Spotlight for this lesson is on the *th* consonant chunk. In modern English, the letters *th* make three different sounds: the soft sound in *thin*, the voiced sound in *then*, and the *t* sound in *Thomas*. You may want to ask your student to think of other words with each sound of *th*. The first two sounds are fairly common, but the third may be more challenging. Two examples are *Thailand* and *thyme*. The combination *th* also appears together in words such as *anthill*, where the letters are parts of two different syllables, and each is pronounced with its own syllable: *ant-hill*.

## Lesson 6: Great Pyramid (Vowel and Consonant Chunks)

- This lesson continues to review vowel and consonant chunks.

- The Spotlight for this lesson features the word *limestone*. If you wish, challenge your student to think of other compound words that contain either *lime* or *stone*. Examples are *limeade, limelight, milestone, rhinestone,* and *sandstone*.

- The area of the base of the Great Pyramid is a little less than 10 football fields. You could also say that it is almost the same as three average-size city blocks. The length of one side is 756 feet.

## Lesson 7: Rubber Balls (Bossy *r* Chunks)

- This lesson introduces Bossy *r* chunks. When a vowel (*a, e, i, o, u*) is followed by an *r*, the vowel sound changes (that is, the *r* "bosses" the vowel).

- Have your student read the following word pairs: *cat-car, bed-her, sit-sir, hot-for, pup-purr.* Point out how the vowel makes its regular short sound in the first word but changes in the second word as it is affected by the *r*.

- Have your student use purple to mark the Bossy *r* chunks in the passage.

- Why words with similar sounds are spelled differently can seem like a mystery. However, people who study the history of words often find clues that explain the reasons behind the spellings. For example, the word *century* is related to the Latin word *centum*, which means *hundred*, and it has kept its *u* even though other parts of the word have changed.

- Here are some words that end with a Bossy *r* chunk and the letter *y*: *primary, salary (ar* chunks*); artery, battery, mystery, pottery (er* chunks*); factory, history, memory, victory (or* chunks*); century, injury (ur* chunks*)*. If you wish, copy each word onto a note card and have your student sort the words according to the Bossy *r* chunk in each one.

## Lesson 8: Trojan Horse (Bossy *r* Chunks)

- This lesson provides more practice with Bossy *r* chunks. Be sure to have your student mark the chunks on his copywork as well as on the printed passage.

- The *Iliad* and the *Odyssey* are famous stories credited to a blind poet named Homer. No one knows if Homer was a real person, but his stories have been loved and handed down for many generations. The story of the Trojan horse is part of the *Iliad*.

- The word *conquer* comes to us from Latin through Old French. Vowel combinations that are less common in English often signal a French root.

## Lesson 9: Phoenicians (Vowel, Consonant, and Bossy *r* Chunks)

- In Lesson 9, your student will be marking all three letter combinations studied so far. Be sure that the correct color is used for each chunk.

- This lesson includes the words *carried* and *borrowed*. The student should mark the Bossy *r* chunk (*ar, or*), rather than the consonant chunk (*rr*) in each word. However, it is not incorrect to mark the consonant chunk. The goal of chunking is to teach the student to look closely at words, so if she chooses a different pattern than the one marked in the Answer Key, point out the alternate possibility and move on.

- The Spotlight features the *ph* consonant chunk. Many words with this combination have Greek roots. Learning the meaning of these roots can be helpful in understanding unfamiliar words. For example, the Greek root *phone* means *sound*. If you wish, see if your student can match these words with their meanings: *phonics*—"the science of sound," *telephone*—"far sound," and *symphony*—"together sound."

- You may also want to point out to your student that our word *alphabet* comes from the first two letters of the Greek alphabet—*alpha* and *beta*.

- Be sure to limit the time spent on copywork or dictation to 10 minutes each day. If the student does not finish the passage, do not worry. Move on to a new page the next day. Your student will have many opportunities to practice the words in other contexts.

### Lesson 10: First Olympics (Vowel, Consonant, and Bossy *r* Chunks)

- This lesson continues to review vowel, consonant, and Bossy *r* chunks.

- *Etymology* is the study of the origin and development of words. Some students may want to look up the history of words that they find interesting. Be sure to keep this word study interest-based for now. (Do not confuse *etymology* with *entomology*, which is the study of insects.)

### Lesson 11: Hanging Gardens (Tricky *y* Guy)

- The letter *y* is usually a consonant (*year, yak*), but sometimes it is "tricky" and sounds like a vowel. Tricky *y* Guy is usually found at the end of words, where it can sound like long *e* (*lady*) or long *i* (*fly*). Use green to mark Tricky *y* Guy.

- Sometimes Tricky *y* Guy appears in the middle of a word. It may sound like short *i* (as in *bicycle*), long *e* (as in *everybody*), or long *i* (as in *flying*). When *y* is the first letter of either a word or a syllable, it is not tricky. Instead, it keeps its regular consonant sound.

- The word *extremely* has a Tricky *y* Guy at the end. In Lesson 12, the student will be asked to mark the *-ly* ending in *usually* instead of the Tricky *y* Guy. However, since endings are not included in this lesson, it is fine to mark the *y* in *extremely* as a Tricky *y* Guy.

- The Spotlight features words related to *beauty*. Here are some other interesting words with the *eau* letter pattern: *bureau*—chest of drawers or government office, *bureaucrat*—someone who works in a government office, *chateau*—an imposing home, often in France, *plateau*—high, relatively flat land, *Juneau*—the capital of Alaska; named after prospector Joe Juneau. All of these words have French roots.

### Lesson 12: Great Wall of China (Endings)

- Unlike a consonant chunk, an ending contains individual sounds that you may be able to hear separately if you pronounce them carefully. The endings that should be identified are listed on the student pages. Have your student find the endings and mark them in pink or red.

- The Spotlight for this lesson calls attention to words with the *-ed* ending. Four of the verbs in the passage (*attacked, mixed, packed,* and *called*) have the *-ed* added without any other changes. Two of the verbs (*forced* and *continued*) are different because the final *e* was dropped before the ending was added.

- There are several different patterns for adding endings to words. They will be presented in more detail in the next level of Spelling You See. For now, call your student's attention to the fact that interesting things can happen with endings. A student's visual memory should tell him that *forceed* and *continueed* are incorrect spellings.

- When guiding dictation, do not tell the student to "sound out" a word. Instead, remind her of another word that has the same letter combination. On the D dictation page, you may simply tell her the troublesome letters. Remember to limit the time spent on dictation to 10 minutes a day.

## Lesson 13: Lighthouse of Alexandria (Silent Letters)

- Some words have silent letters that are not part of vowel chunks, consonant chunks, or endings. Silent *e* is most common and is often found at the end of a word. Other words, such as *could* and *would,* have a silent *l*. Notice that the silent *l* may change the sound of the vowel, just as Bossy *r* does. Some words have a silent *b* or a silent *h*. Examples of words with these silent letters are *thumb, John*, and *oh*.

- Have your student mark the silent letters in orange. He should not mark silent letters that are part of the letter patterns he has already learned.

- The Lighthouse of Alexandria was about 400 feet high—about the same as an average 40-story building.

- Some compound words ending with house are *birdhouse, clubhouse, farmhouse, greenhouse, schoolhouse*, and *storehouse*. Your student may think of others.

- Silent letters can give us clues about a word's history, but they also help make meaning and pronunciation clear. Challenge your student to find three words in the passage for this lesson that change pronunciation and meaning when the silent *e* is removed. The words are *one, fire*, and *huge*. Without the silent *e*, they become, respectively, *on, fir,* and *hug*.

## Lesson 14: Athens and Democracy (All Letter Patterns)

- For Lessons 14-18, your student will continue to mark all six letter patterns that have been presented. It is important to continue using the suggested color for each pattern. This will imprint the correct spellings on the visual memory and also make it easier to compare the student's work with the **Answer Key**.

- The words *citizen* and *democracy* both come from the Greek language. There are many related words that also have to do with government. The Spotlight in the *Student Workbook* describes some of them. There are also many interesting words that have the same ending as *democracy*. The word *democracy* means "rule of the people." *Aristocracy* means "rule by aristocrats," and *autocracy* means "rule by one person."

## Lesson 15: Chariot Races (All Letter Patterns)

- Examples of compound words ending in *time* are *bedtime, daytime, downtime, lunchtime, mealtime, nighttime, playtime, ragtime*, and *springtime*. Examples of compound words beginning with *some* are *someday, somehow, someone, something, somewhat*, and *somewhere*. If your student suggests other examples, you may want to check a dictionary to see if the phrase should be written as one word, hyphenated, or written as two words.

- The *-ly* ending is often used to change an adjective to an adverb. An adjective describes, or modifies, a noun, as in "*wild* fans." An adverb describes, or modifies, a verb, as in "The fans cheered *wildly*." If you wish, read the following sentences to your student and ask her to fill in the blanks with adverbs from this week's passage. Fierce men fought _____. (*fiercely*) Wild fans cheered _____. (*wildly*) Thick dust rose _____. (*thickly*)

## Lesson 16: Roman Roads (All Letter Patterns)

- Continue to limit the time spent on copywork and dictation to 10 minutes and allow the student to move on to a new page the next day.

- The two words that rhyme with *built* and have the same letter pattern are *guilt* and *quilt*. Students probably already know that the letter *q* is regularly followed by *u* in English.

- One-syllable words that rhyme with *built* but do not have the *u* are *gilt, hilt, jilt, kilt, lilt, silt, spilt, stilt, tilt*, and *wilt*.

### Lesson 17: Rice Terraces (All Letter Patterns)

- Several words in this lesson end with the letters *-es*. They are *Philippines, sides, pipes,* and *terraces*. All of these are formed from words that end in *e*. Students may have learned that many plurals are formed by adding *-s* or *-es* to the base word. The structure of the base word determines how this is done. Because the emphasis of this program is on visual memory of words, the student is asked to mark the *-es* as an ending, even though it looks as though only the *-s* was added. As with the *-ed* ending, your student should be able to see that *pipees* and *sidees* are incorrect spellings.

### Lesson 18: Dead Sea Scrolls (All Letter Patterns)

- With this lesson, your student will have finished *Ancient Achievements, Part 1*. Be sure to celebrate this accomplishment.

- The Mediterranean Sea is the "sea in the middle of the land." A look at a map makes it clear why it was given this name.

### Lesson 19: Colosseum (All Letter Patterns: Split Review)

- Welcome to *Ancient Achievements, Part 2*. Your student will continue to mark the letter patterns, or chunks, that were introduced in *Ancient Achievements, Part 1*. The first several lessons in this book will divide the review of the chunks into two parts. Your student should mark vowel chunks, consonant chunks, and Bossy *r* chunks on the first three days of the lesson; on the last two days, he will be directed to mark Tricky *y* Guy, endings, and silent letters.

- You may notice that some letters are marked differently, depending on what the student is instructed to look for on that day. Remember that the purpose is not to teach the structure of the English language but to develop a visual memory for how words are spelled.

- A modern arena is usually a place for relatively peaceful sports events. However, the original Latin word means "place of combat."

- The Spotlight mentions the word *colossal* as describing something very large. Your student might enjoy trying to think of other words that have a similar meaning, such as *enormous, gargantuan, gigantic, huge, immense, mammoth, massive, vast,* and *voluminous*. Challenge your student to choose one of these words and use it in conversation today.

## Lesson 20: Chinese Printing (All Letter Patterns: Split Review)

- This lesson continues to review chunking by having the student mark three of the patterns he has learned on worksheets A, B, and C and the other three patterns on worksheets D and E.

- The Spotlight introduces the term *affix*. An affix may be added to the beginning or the end of a word. *Suffixes* and *prefixes* are different kinds of affixes. They may make a noun plural, change the tense of a verb, change a word to a different part of speech, or give a word an opposite meaning. Your student may learn about some of these functions in her other studies. For this course, just call your student's attention to the power of these little pieces of words and encourage her to notice how they are attached to the original words.

- In the Spotlight, the student is asked what happens to the final *e* in *challenge* when the affix is added. He should see that it is dropped rather than included. Again, the student's experience in marking word endings and his visual memory should tell him that *challengeed* is not correctly spelled.

## Lesson 21: Artillery (All Letter Patterns: Split Review)

- Notice that this lesson continues the split review of chunking patterns, with vowel chunks, consonant chunks, and Bossy *r* chunks being marked on the first three days and Tricky *y* Guy, endings, and silent letters being marked on the last two days.

- Related words can give important clues about spelling. The Spotlight discusses the relationships between *native* and *nation* and between *tense* and *tension*. Here are some more word pairs that can help the student spell words with the *shun* sound: *act—action, discuss—discussion, relative—relation, express—expression.*

- The compound word in the passage is *gunpowder*. Continue to call attention to compound words whenever you find them.

## Lesson 22: Timbuktu (All Letter Patterns: Split Review)

- This lesson continues to review chunking. The student will mark three of the letter patterns on worksheets A, B, and C and three different patterns on worksheets D and E.

- Your student may see alternate spellings of *Timbuktu*. There is disagreement about what the word means. Some think it refers to a hollow in the sandy hills.

- *Kalamazoo* is a city in Michigan. Its name comes from an old Native American word. Again, people disagree about what the word actually means.

## Lesson 23: King Arthur (All Letter Patterns: Split Review)

- This lesson continues the split review of the chunking patterns.

- Remember that the student should not spend more than 10 minutes a day on copywork or dictation. Short, unstressful writing times are actually more effective than longer sessions that become unpleasant to the student.

- Some other common words with the *kn* consonant chunk are *knife, knit, knee, knot, knob*, and *knock*. If you wish, ask your student to examine these words and decide which ones would still be meaningful without the initial letter *k*. They are *nit* (a louse egg), *not*, *nob* (slang for the human head), and *nock* (the notch on a bow).

- The compound words in this passage are *whoever* and *noblemen*.

## Lesson 24: Zero (All Letter Patterns: Split Review)

- This is the last lesson that will split the review of the letter patterns.

- Other words in English that have the idea of nothing are *nil, naught* (or *nought*), and *zilch*. When numbers are being read aloud, the words *oh* and *aught* are sometimes used for the zero, even though neither word actually means the same as zero.

## Lesson 25: Vikings (All Letter Patterns)

- For the rest of the lessons in this book, the student will be asked to mark all of the letter patterns each day.

- If you wish, challenge your student to find the six compound words in the passage: *shipbuilders, longships, highways, coastline, lightweight*, and *sometimes*. As has been noted before, some related words are written as two words, some are written as a single word, and a few are hyphenated.

  - *Shipbuilder, shipwreck*, and *shipyard* are all written as one word.

- *Longship, steamship, airship*, and *flagship* are each single words, but *cruise ship* is written as two words. Most phrases beginning with *long* are written as two words. Exceptions are *longhand, longbow,* and *longshoreman.*

- *Lightweight* is a single word. Phrases beginning with *light* are usually written as two words, but the single word *lighthouse* is an exception, and *light-year* is often written with a hyphen.

- *Highway* is a single word, *high school* is two words, and *high-pitched* is a written with a hyphen.

- *Coastline* is a single word, *bus line* is two words, and *half-line* is written with a hyphen.

- There is a discussion of compound words related to *sometimes* in Lesson 15.

- Encourage your student to notice compound words as she completes the chunking and copywork activities so that she develops a visual memory for how they are written. When she is writing in other contexts, you may want to help her use a dictionary or the internet to see how a phrase should be written.

## Lesson 26: Charlemagne (All Letter Patterns)

- *Charlemagne* is pronounced *"SHAR le mane."* The *g* and the final *e* are silent.

- A simpler word related to *magnificent* is *magnify*. It means "to make larger."

- Charlemagne encouraged teaching the seven traditional subjects of a classical education in his schools. Those subjects are grammar (the study of language), rhetoric (persuasive speech), logic, arithmetic, geometry, music, and astronomy. Students who use the classical method of learning are following in the footsteps of Charlemagne.

## Lesson 27: Gunpowder (All Letter Patterns)

- Remember that the dictation exercise is not a test. Always count the number of words spelled correctly and help your student see the progress he is making.

- The *-ly* ending is commonly used to change an adjective to an adverb. An *explosive* device will go off *explosively*. Encourage your student to look closely at how adding an ending affects the spelling of a word.

- The compound word in this passage is *gunpowder*.

- Your student may be interested to know that the Chinese developed a peaceful use for gunpowder as well. They are credited with the invention of fireworks.

## Lesson 28: Lalibela (All Letter Patterns)

- Continue to have your student read the passage aloud each day before she marks it. Be sure to help her with the pronunciation or meaning of any unfamiliar words.

- Some students are fascinated by the ways that people from different countries are named in English. (For example, the French are the people of France.) If your student is interested and you are willing to do some research, you may wish to play a geography game. One game involves a globe. Have your student spin the globe, put his finger on a country, and try to name the people of the country. Many will be familiar. If you or your student do not know the correct name, look it up or make a list of names to look up later.

- You can also make two sets of cards with country names on one set and the names of the inhabitants on the other set. Shuffle each set of cards and see how quickly your student can match the names of the countries with the names of the people who live there.

## Lesson 29: Knights (All Letter Patterns)

- Keep the dictation exercises positive. Count the number of words written correctly each time, rather than the number written incorrectly.

- Some words that rhyme with *knight* and contain the *gh* consonant chunk are *fight, flight, light,* and *sight*. Without the *gh*, the words become *fit, flit, lit,* and *sit*. The new spellings are recognizable words, but your student should notice how the vowel sound changes.

## Lesson 30: Leeches (All Letter Patterns)

- There are many words that rhyme with *leech*. Two of them with the same vowel chunk are *speech* and *screech*. Some rhyming words with the *ea* vowel chunk are *bleach, peach, reach,* and *teach.*

## Lesson 31: Longbow (All Letter Patterns)

- Most students know that a *q* is usually followed by a *u*. Occasionally, you or your student may see an apparent exception. Two of them are mentioned in this week's Spotlight. *Qatar* is a small country on the Arabian Peninsula. The name *Qatar* is an attempt to translate the pronunciation from Arabic to English. Strictly speaking, it is not an English word and does not follow English language rules.

- *Qantas* is an Australian airline. Its name is made up from the initials for "*Q*ueensland *a*nd *N*orthern *T*erritory *A*erial *S*ervices."

- The four compound words found in this passage are *outlaw, longbow, bowstring,* and *Sundays.*

## Lesson 32: Leaning Tower of Pisa (All Letter Patterns)

- Continue to limit the time spent on copywork or dictation to 10 minutes a day. It is better for a student to write fewer words correctly than to write many words with errors.

- The nouns *fame, danger*, and *mystery* all become adjectives with the addition of the letters -*ous*. Encourage your student to see that the ending is added to the word *danger* without any changes. On the other hand, the final *e* in *fame* is dropped when the ending is added, and the final *y* in mystery is changed to *i* before the addition of -*ous*.

- Some other adjectives ending in -*ous* are *enormous, numerous, religious, serious, tremendous, obvious,* and *various*. In some cases, the base word is fairly clear, although the endings are added in different ways. In other cases, the original word is not so clear. Etymologists love to study the backgrounds of words like these, as they offer interesting clues to the history of our language.

### Lesson 33: Inca and Quipus (All Letter Patterns)

- An alternate spelling for *quipus* is *khipus.*

- Marking consonant chunks will develop a strong visual memory for words with double consonants before an ending. The next level of Spelling You See will explore endings in more detail.

- If your student is interested, you can explain the *one-one-one rule.* In general, when an ending such as *-ed, -es,* or *-ing* is added to a **one**-syllable word with **one** vowel followed by **one** consonant, the final consonant is doubled before adding the ending. There are exceptions to the one-one-one rule. For example, the letters *x* and *w* are never doubled when adding endings, so *tax + ed* is *taxed,* and *show + ing* is *showing.* This is why the development of visual memory is so important. A strong visual memory will give the student immediate feedback when an exceptional spelling appears.

### Lesson 34: Magna Carta (All Letter Patterns)

- Common words beginning with *gua* are *guarantee, guard,* and *guardian.* If you wish, work with your student to see how many more words can be made by adding endings to the words in this list.

- *Garden* is an example of a word that has the same beginning sound as *guard* but does not share the *gua* letter pattern.

### Lesson 35: Marco Polo (All Letter Patterns)

- If your student is interested, you can share the following information about the names of the months. The Roman calendar originally began with the planting season in the month of March. The first four months were *Martius, Aprilis, Maius,* and *Iunius.* Three of those months were named after Roman gods, while the origin of *Aprilis* is uncertain. The next six months had number names: *Quintilis, Sextilis, September, October, November,* and *December.* Later, the months of *January* and *February* were named. Finally, *Quintilis* was renamed in honor of Julius Caesar and became our July. *Sextilis* was renamed August in honor of the Emperor Augustus. The calendar that we use today reflects the Roman names but begins with January, so the "tenth month" of December is now actually the twelfth month.

## Lesson 36: Aztecs (All Letter Patterns)

- This is the last lesson of *Ancient Achievements*. Be sure to congratulate your student on a job well done.

- At this point, students should have a strong visual memory for a wide vocabulary of everyday words. They should also have developed the habit of looking closely at words and noticing unusual spelling patterns.

- The next level of Spelling You See will move students into the Word Extension stage of spelling. Students will be using a variety of activities to learn how prefixes and suffixes can change the spelling and meaning of words.

# Weekly Activity Guide

## Guided Reading

A student using *Ancient Achievements* should be an established reader, but it is still important to have the student read the passage aloud each day. As students become more familiar with the passage, they are developing a visual memory for new vocabulary and for irregular spellings. The same passage is used all week to encourage numerous readings.

## Chunking

Chunking is the process of locating and marking specific letter patterns within the passage. At first, students search for one particular kind of letter pattern, or chunk, such as vowel chunks or consonant chunks. Gradually, students are challenged to find and mark multiple spelling patterns in each passage. Students should use colored pencils or highlighters to chunk the passages. The use of color simplifies the process of counting different chunks and adds an element of fun.

The various letter groups are listed below, along with the color that should be used to mark each group.

### Vowel Chunks (yellow)

| | | | | | | | |
|---|---|---|---|---|---|---|---|
| aa | ae | ai | ao | au | aw | ay | |
| ea | ee | ei | eo | eu | ew | ey | eau |
| ia | ie | ii | io | iu | | | |
| oa | oe | oi | oo | ou | ow | oy | |
| ua | ue | ui | uo | uu | uy | | |

- Notice that the three-letter combination *eau* is included in this list.

- Because the letters *w* and *y* can act like vowels, they are also included in some of the vowel chunks.

- Even if each vowel sound is articulated in a vowel pair, as in *radio* or *area*, the pair should be marked as a vowel chunk.

## Consonant Chunks (blue)

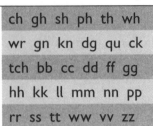

- Notice that the three-letter combination *tch* is included in this list.

- The chunk *qu* is a consonant-vowel combination that we have chosen to include with the consonant chunks.

- In a blend, each letter can be heard making its expected sound. The letter pairs *tw* (*two*) and *sc* (*science*) are treated as blends rather than consonant chunks because they usually are sounded individually (*twig, scope*).

- The combination *mb* is not considered a consonant chunk because each letter is part of a different syllable in many English words (*combine, steamboat*).

## Bossy *r* Chunks (purple)

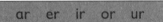

- Notice how the *r* changes the sound of the vowel in the following word pairs: *cat-car, bed-her, sit-sir, hot-for, pup-purr*.

- There are some words (*cupboard, their, your*) that have a vowel chunk followed by a Bossy *r* chunk. If a student is marking both vowel chunks and Bossy *r* chunks in a lesson, we suggest marking the vowel chunk.

- If there is a Bossy *r* chunk before a consonant chunk (*stirrup, hurry*), we suggest marking the Bossy *r* chunk.

## Tricky *y* Guy (green)

- Tricky *y* Guy is usually found at the end of words but may be in the middle. It can sound like long *e* (*baby*), long *i* (*fly*), or short *i* (*bicycle*).

## Endings (pink or red)

| -ed | -es | -ful | -ing | -ly |
|-----|-----|------|------|-----|

- If the student marks *-ly* as an ending in a word like *only*, do not mark it wrong, even though it is not technically an ending added to a base word. Base words and endings are included in advanced word study.

- The *est* and *en* letter combinations frequently appear at the end of words (*west, ten*) as part of the root word. They have not been listed as endings.

- In words such as *doing* and *being*, we suggest marking the endings rather than vowel chunks when the student is looking for both patterns.

## Silent Letters (orange)

- Silent *e* is often found at the end of words. Some words have a silent *b* (*thumb*) or silent *h* (*oh*).

- The *l* in some words (*walk, could*) is silent. Notice that the *l* in *walk* controls the vowel sound of the *a* that precedes it.

- Only silent letters that are not part of chunks should be marked.

## Overlapping Chunks

Some words have overlapping chunks. In words where the final *y* is changed to *i* before adding an ending (*studied, countries*), marking either the ending or the vowel chunk is acceptable. The word *finally* has a consonant chunk (*ll*) and an ending (*-ly*) that overlap. If the focus of the lesson is consonant chunks, students should chunk *ll*. If the focus is endings, students should chunk *-ly*.

In lessons with multiple chunks, vowel chunks are marked before Bossy *r* chunks, but Bossy *r* chunks before consonant chunks. The purpose of chunking is to train the student to look carefully at how words are spelled. If he chooses a different combination of letters than in the answer key, do not mark it wrong. Discuss his choice and point out other possibilities. Your student may find it helpful to chunk the letter combination that he thinks will be the most difficult to remember.

## Copywork

On Days 1–3 (Parts A–C), the student is asked to copy the passage on the right-hand page. The student should feel free to erase if a word is accidentally spelled incorrectly. Allow the student to stop copying after 10 minutes. After the time is up, the student should chunk his work (mark the letter patterns), looking at the opposite page if needed.

English does not use phonics rules consistently because it developed from many different languages. Copywork is therefore very important in helping students learn our language. Students take words in visually and then copy them kinesthetically. Throughout the process, they also must pay close attention to details in print that might otherwise elude them. Copywork acts as a cognitive structuring device, sorting information visually so it is more easily organized and processed by the brain. Recopying the same passage several times leads to familiarity with common letter patterns, as well as with non-phonetic words that are often difficult for students.

Do not allow students to use cursive for copywork or dictation. They need to be able to make a visual connection with printed words in the books they read. Save penmanship practice for another time.

## Spotlight

On Day 3 (Part C), there is a special feature called a Spotlight, which is designed to stimulate curiosity about words and begin to prepare students for Word Extension, the next stage of spelling. There is more information about the Spotlights in the lesson-by-lesson section of the *Instructor's Handbook*. Some lessons include suggestions for additional activities. Discuss the information in the Spotlight with your student, but do not put pressure on your student to complete the activities.

## First Dictation

Dictation is not a stand-alone activity. Students should always chunk the passage in Section 1 first, which helps them learn how to learn, how to store information, how to create links, and how to remember. This sets them up for success. Neurologically, students must be relaxed, engaged, and motivated. They should consider dictation a game or a challenge. Be positive and always count the number of words spelled correctly, not the number spelled incorrectly.

Cover the left-hand page in the workbook with a piece of paper and read the story from the **Resources** section of this *Handbook*. Help the student to relax and let her know that the dictation will only last for 10 minutes. Provide punctuation and capitalization if needed, and help the student with difficult words. Read the passage slowly until your student needs assistance. Stop to help, but don't stop the clock, as it is important to address misspellings as they occur without worrying about time. The goal is quality, not quantity. It is more beneficial for students to write each word correctly than to write many words incorrectly.

Discuss the non-phonetic word parts – the "rule breakers" – as you go. For example, show students how tricky the *gh* chunk is. This consonant chunk appears in words like *light*, *enough*, and *ghost*. *Ugh*! The *ai* chunk appears in *rain*, *again*, *said*, and *captain*. The word *house* has a silent *e* at the end, just to make it "look right." This is why it is not helpful to tell students to use phonics rules to "sound it out." When we show them that the rules are inconsistent, we relieve them of the burden of figuring out why a word is spelled a certain way. Their brains are then free to continue visualizing the word in context and retrieving that visual image from memory.

## Second Dictation

The second weekly dictation exercise is a little different than the first. Don't forget to have the student chunk the passage first. Then the student should attempt to write the passage from dictation without any assistance other than with capitalization and punctuation, if needed. Even though the student is encouraged to write independently, be very clear that this is not a test. Explain to your student that her paper is "sloppy copy" and that she does not need to erase. Because students sometimes have to write words several ways before they pinpoint the one that looks right, it is critical to let them compare different spellings. You may prompt her by saying, "Try it with and without an *e* at the end." Have her draw a line through the wrong word and keep going. After 10 minutes, stop dictating and have the student check her work by comparing it with the original passage. Then count and record the number of words that were spelled correctly. Always be positive and emphasize this number, not the number of words that are incorrect. As time goes on, you should see an improvement in the number of words that are spelled correctly each week.

# Frequently Asked Questions

1.  **Are students allowed to ask for help?**
    Yes. The purpose is to help the student learn to spell. If your student writes a word incorrectly during the first weekly dictation exercise, help him right away before moving on. Don't stop the clock. Each time a word is written correctly, it is more likely to be remembered. On the second weekly dictation page, encourage your student to work more independently.

2.  **In lessons where chunks overlap, which one should my student mark?**
    Some words will have overlapping chunks or letter patterns. In general, we suggest marking vowel chunks before Bossy *r* chunks, Bossy *r* chunks before consonant chunks, and endings before silent letters. However, since the purpose of chunking is to encourage students to notice spelling patterns and to develop a visual memory, do not consider different choices wrong. Instead, discuss the other options that the student may have chosen. You may want to ask the student which letter pattern she thinks would be most helpful for her to remember and let her mark that one. Look at **Chunking** on page 33 for more information.

3.  **My daughter wants to do her copywork in cursive. Is this okay?**
    No. Copywork should be printed in order to develop visual memory. When students read, everything they see is in print, so they should use printing while learning to spell.

4.  **Should I be concerned about careful handwriting?**
    The focus of this course is on spelling, not handwriting. Allow the student to write quickly and efficiently. Words should be legible, but intensive handwriting practice should be saved for another time.

5.  **Should my student erase during copywork or passage dictation?**
    Students should erase during copywork if necessary so that they copy the words correctly. When students are completing dictation, however, it is important not to erase. Give your student the chance to write the word multiple times, if needed, in order to see which one looks right. Simply have him draw a line through the incorrect words.

6. **How important is it for my student to complete the activities connected with the weekly Spotlights?**

   The Spotlights are designed to stimulate curiosity about words and to introduce students to concepts that they will encounter in the next two stages of spelling. We encourage you to read and discuss the Spotlights with your student. However, let the student's interest level determine how much time you spend on the Spotlight activities in the *Student Workbook* or the *Handbook*.

7. **Should I keep a list of words that my student misses?**

   No, this is not necessary. Commonly-misspelled words will come up again in future lessons. This program encourages visual memory, not rote memory.

8. **There are no spelling tests with this program. How can I tell if my child is making progress?**

   Look for increased accuracy and speed in completing a dictation page. You should also see more accurate spelling in other daily work. However, remember that each child will progress through the developmental process at his own pace, so be patient and do not put pressure on your student. Dictation exercises should not be treated as tests. Regardless of how a student performs on the final dictation of the week, always move forward to a new passage on the next week. If you are required or would like to keep a portfolio of your student's work, pages may be removed from the workbooks at regular intervals and kept in a folder to demonstrate progress.

9. **We didn't have time to do spelling every day this week. Is it important to finish every worksheet?**

   While it is important to work on spelling consistently, it should not be a burden to you or your student. Feel free to start a new lesson each week, even if the previous lesson was not completed. The common words and letter patterns will be repeated many times throughout the course.

10. **My daughter does fine in her spelling book and when she's copying word for word. If she writes something on her own, though, her spelling is horrible. Why?**

    Copying and creating are two very different activities for the brain. Copywork and dictation help the student develop a visual memory, as the brain is focusing on the way the words actually look in print. When she is creating a story, her brain is operating differently. It takes a long time for spelling to become implanted and automatic. Until that happens, you will continue to see spelling errors in her free writing. That is why consistent copying of the same passage multiple times is so critical.

# Resources

## Passages for Dictation

**1**  The Cave of Lascaux is one of the most famous caves in the world. One day four French teenagers were exploring. When the boys eased into a hidden cave, they were shocked! It was painted! Bison, deer, horses, cows, and bulls seemed to leap across the cave walls and ceilings. Some pictures showed people hunting animals. Thousands of years before, ancient people had painted these pictures. They had used minerals to make paints. They left behind a visual treasure.

**2**  An airplane was flying over the German countryside near Goseck. The pilot saw a large circle in the wheat fields below. People had noticed similar circles before. Their purpose was a mystery. A group of young archeologists studied the Goseck Circle. They found four circles inside each other. One was a mound, and one was a ditch. Two of them were once marked with wooden fences. The gates in the fences lined up with the sun on certain days of the year. The circles may have helped people keep track of the seasons.

**3**  Thousands of years ago, the Sumerians created a system of writing. It is called cuneiform. That's an odd name, but it actually makes sense. The name comes from the Latin word *cuneus*. It means *wedge*. The Sumerians used a wedge-shaped writing tool. They pressed this tool into damp clay tablets. Then the tablets were baked in the scorching sun. Writing was not the quick and easy process it is today. Some tablets lasted a long time. As a result, we know more about how people lived long ago.

**4**  The ancient Chinese had a secret. A person who shared the secret with others might be killed. This hidden knowledge started with a moth and a tree. Each moth laid eggs that produced silkworms. Each silkworm ate mulberry leaves. The worm produced a long, thin thread. The thread formed a cocoon. Women learned to harvest the cocoons at just the right time. They wove the threads into fine silk. For centuries, the Chinese guarded this secret. They traded their precious silk for other valuable products.

**5**   Ancient Egyptians believed it was important not to let a body decay after death. Rich people preserved bodies with great care. First, the brain was removed and discarded as worthless. Some organs were saved in jars. The heart was left in the body. To Egyptians, the heart was the center of reason. They washed the body and packed it in salts to dry. Weeks later, they wrapped it in cloth. Finally, they placed this mummy in a special coffin. The coffin was placed inside one or more larger coffins.

**6**   "Time laughs at all things, but the pyramids laugh at time." That old saying seems true. Some pyramids have lasted so long they must be laughing! The Great Pyramid in Egypt was built thousands of years ago. Many other famous buildings are gone, but the Great Pyramid remains. It is massive. Its base covers 13 acres. It contains more than two million limestone and granite blocks. Some of the blocks weigh over two tons. It was built to house the pharaoh's body forever.

**7**   The first rubber balls were made in Central America. People learned how to gather the sap of the rubber tree. They mixed the sap with the juice of the morning glory vine. When the rubber hardened, it could be used to make many things. Rubber balls were used for games. Many years later, explorers found some of these balls. However, the exact rules of the games are still a mystery.

**8**   The Greeks told stories about a war with Troy. After fighting for ten years, both sides were tired of the war. The Greeks made a clever plan. They built an enormous wooden horse. Their best warriors hid inside. The Greeks wheeled the horse to the gates of Troy and pretended to sail away. The people of Troy thought it was a gift. They wheeled the Trojan horse into their city. That was a major blunder! During the night, the Greek warriors slipped out of the Trojan horse and conquered Troy. The story of the Trojan War is still told today.

**9**  The Phoenicians lived near the sea. They built sturdy ships and sailed around the ancient world trading goods. Their ships carried olive oil and cedar wood to other ports. They sold purple dye and metalwork. As they sailed, they spread their alphabet. It used letters instead of pictures. The Greeks borrowed the alphabet and made some changes. The Romans changed it even more. A few letters in our alphabet still remind us of these older letters.

**10**  Ancient Greece was made up of city-states. People were fiercely loyal to their city-state. They were often at war with other city-states. Once a year they called a truce. Men gathered to compete in foot races. Every four years they met in Olympia for special events. These early Olympics grew to include sports such as boxing and wrestling. Later, events with horses were added. Women were allowed to compete in those events. The winners brought honor to their city-states.

**11**  A story from long ago tells about a king who married a woman from a far country. The woman became homesick for her own country. She missed the beauty of its green hills and mountains. The king's country was extremely hot, flat, and dry. The king decided to build his wife a garden as high as a mountain. Workers used bricks and stones to build it. They added terraces filled with soil, trees, and flowers. Storytellers called the king's gift the Hanging Gardens of Babylon. Ruins of gardens have been found in dry places.

**12**  China was often attacked by tribes living to the north. One king built a stone wall even before China was an empire. The first Chinese emperor forced his people to build a wall. They mixed sand, gravel, and clay. This mixture was then packed into place. Wall building continued for many centuries. The walls usually didn't stop enemies. However, they were helpful in slowing down an army. The most famous wall is called the Great Wall of China. You can still see parts of this wall winding over hills and valleys.

**13** Lighthouses have guided ships for centuries. One famous lighthouse was built at Alexandria, Egypt. It was about 400 feet high. Its purpose was to help ships find the harbor. What type of light shone in this lighthouse thousands of years ago? Fire! Light from this fire guided ships at night. Some people wrote that smoke could be seen during the day. Others believe that a huge mirror reflected the sun during the day. This lighthouse was a beacon to ships and a symbol of Alexandria.

**14** Thousands of years ago, the people of Athens tried something new. They didn't want to be ruled by one person or family. They created a new form of government. Citizens met often to discuss and debate. They made the laws. They also served in office. Only free men over 18 were citizens. Our word democracy comes from two Greek words. *Demos* means the common people of a country. *Kratos* means rule. In a democracy, the people rule.

**15** Chariot races were popular in ancient Greece. Horses burst from the starting gates. Men standing in chariots whipped their horses fiercely. The frenzy began! Fans cheered wildly for their favorite teams. Hooves thundered. Whips cracked. Dust rose thickly from the racetrack. At the turns, chariots often crashed into each other or into the side walls. Sometimes teams ran over the wrecked chariots. This kind of racing was a very risky sport!

**16** The Roman Empire grew in size and power over many centuries. It's no wonder! Its large army was a fighting machine. Soldiers were well trained and well organized. As they conquered more and more people, they acquired more and more land. The army built a system of roads throughout the vast empire. This helped soldiers travel quickly. They preferred to build straight roads. After all, marching around curves took more time! Roman roads were well built. Some of them lasted longer than the Empire.

**17** Two thousand years ago in the Philippines, some people faced a challenge. How could they farm the steep mountainsides where they lived? They planned and worked. They built walls of mud and stone. They created terraces along the sides of the mountains. A system of bamboo pipes was used to carry water down from the forest on top of the mountain. At first they grew a plant called taro. Later, each terrace became a rice paddy. With vision and hard work, they met the challenge of the mountain.

**18** Some of the world's treasures have been found by accident. One example is the Dead Sea Scrolls. A young man was tending his goats near the rugged shores of the Dead Sea. He noticed one goat was missing. As he searched the rocky terrain, he entered a cave. There he found clay jars with ancient scrolls inside. The scrolls were copies of many old books. Some of them were old copies of parts of the Hebrew Bible. Scholars believe these long-lost scrolls were hidden about 1900 years before they were found.

**19** The Roman Empire had a civil war. There were three emperors in one year! Finally, an army general became emperor. He wanted to keep the people happy. That way they would not want to fight again. He ordered the Colosseum to be built. This building was a very large arena. It was built with concrete and stone. There were many arches for beauty and strength. The places where the emperor and nobles sat were decorated with marble. The ruins of the Colosseum still stand in the middle of Rome.

**20** The Chinese were the first people to print books. Their language uses thousands of characters instead of a simple alphabet. For many years they carved each page into a wooden block. Later, each character was carved from clay. The characters were baked so they would harden. Next they were fastened onto iron plates. A page was printed from each plate. Thankfully the clay characters could be used over and over! The process was a challenge. Still, it was easier than copying books by hand.

**21**  "Ready, aim, throw!" Before gunpowder and cannons were invented, armies used other machines to attack enemies from a distance. Some weapons stored tension in ropes. When the ropes were released, objects were hurled through the air. One weapon shot bolts. These were like arrows but were as big as spears. A different weapon hurled stones and fire over city walls. Later machines were built that could hurl stones as big as cars into castles.

**22**  Timbuktu is a desert city in Africa. Camels carried salt from mines to the city. People traded the salt as well as gold and grain. One year the emperor traveled to Egypt. He spent a great deal of gold. People decided Timbuktu was very rich! Stories about the city also made it sound very mysterious. Scholars knew that the city had another treasure. It had libraries of handwritten books. People visited the city just to study these books.

**23**  Minstrels entertained people by singing ballads and retelling stories. The legends of King Arthur were popular. One story tells about a sword stuck in a stone. Whoever pulled the sword from the stone was the rightful king. Many noblemen had already tried and failed. Young Arthur effortlessly removed the sword. Immediately he was crowned king. He reigned with the help of the Knights of the Round Table. King Arthur might not have been a real person, but the stories are still loved.

**24**  Can you imagine trying to do math without the number zero? Some ancient people used columns to show place value. They wrote a special mark when a column was empty. It kept people from reading the wrong number. Then people in India began to use a symbol as a number that meant "none." Travelers brought this useful new number elsewhere. The idea of zero spread across the world. It opened the door to many new ideas in math.

**25**  The Vikings lived by the North Sea. They became expert shipbuilders. For two centuries, they used their longships to raid the lands around them. The design of the ships made them ideal for the job. They could be used in very shallow water, so the rivers soon became highways to places far from the coastline. Very thin hulls made the ships lightweight and easy to maneuver. A crew of warriors used oars to propel the ship. Sometimes a sail was used as well. Some of the Vikings also made their homes in the lands they had raided.

**26**  When Charlemagne became king, life was difficult. People used most of their energy to grow food and keep safe from enemies. The king thought that books and learning were important. He created places where books could be copied and saved. He started schools where people could learn to read and write. He even tried to learn to read and write for himself. The schools also taught other subjects such as arithmetic and astronomy. Some of the king's ideas about education are still popular today.

**27**  Imagine being on the scene when gunpowder was first discovered. According to old reports, some Chinese men were mixing different substances. They were trying to create a mixture that would prolong life. As they heated their mixture, it began to burn. Suddenly there was an explosion. What a shock! The men were caught off guard. Their hands and faces were badly burned. The place where they were working burned to the ground. It probably didn't take them long to realize their discovery would never prolong life.

**28**  Most buildings are made from many pieces. Can you imagine a building made from just one block of stone? If you travel to Lalibela in Ethiopia, you will see some very old churches. They are carved out of solid rock. Some of them were hewn into the side of a mountain. Others were made by cutting straight down into the rock from the top of a hill. First the outside of the building was cut from the rock. Then the inside was hollowed out. Windows and decorations were also carved. The buildings are about 900 years old. They are still used today.

**29**  During the Middle Ages, knights kept improving their armor. Eventually, they went into battle dressed from head to toe in heavy metal suits. Even their horses were covered in metal armor. This caused a problem. On the battlefield all the knights looked similar. Who was an ally? Who was an enemy? It was hard to tell the difference! Each family designed a unique coat of arms. The knights of that family painted this coat of arms on their armor. A father passed the family coat of arms down to his sons. The problem was solved!

**30**  Does the thought of leeches make you shudder? Leeches are a kind of worm that feeds on blood from other animals. For centuries, physicians believed that some diseases were caused by having too much blood. They often used leeches as a remedy. The leeches attached themselves to a patient's skin. Then they drew blood out of the veins. Leeches produce a substance that prevents blood from clotting. As a result, the blood kept flowing. The leeches kept filling up with blood until they could not hold any more.

**31**  Have you ever heard of Robin Hood? Stories say that he was an outlaw who stole from the rich to help the poor. Robin Hood may only be a legend, but the type of bow he used in the stories was real. The Welsh longbow was a powerful weapon. Drawing the bowstring required a lot of strength. Men needed to practice a long time before they could shoot quickly and accurately. King Edward the Third wanted skilled English archers. He said that every man had to practice with his longbow on Sundays and holidays.

**32**  Why is the Leaning Tower of Pisa so famous? It seems to defy gravity. The building has been leaning for over 800 years. The foundation was not built deeply enough. The soil under it settled unevenly. Years ago people stopped ringing the bells in the tower. Scientists thought the vibrations would make the tower fall. Recent work strengthened the tower while keeping the famous lean. Now the bells are rung again. Visitors can climb nearly 300 steps to the top.

**33**  Different people have recorded information in different ways. Some etched pictures. Some groups of people drew symbols. Some used characters or alphabets to write words. The Incas had a unique system for recording numbers. They tied knots on strings. Different colored strings were attached to a base to keep them organized. Three different types of knots stood for ones, tens, and hundreds. The knotted strings were called quipus. They were used to keep track of data such as work done and taxes paid. Many things about the quipus are still a mystery.

**34**  King John thought that kings were above the law. He taxed the English people heavily. He seized any land that he wanted. He arrested people who disagreed with him. In short, he did whatever he felt like doing. Powerful noblemen grew angry about having a tyrant for their king. Finally they acted. They forced the king to accept the Magna Carta, or Great Charter. This document guaranteed certain rights to free men. King John did not keep the agreement, but the idea of freedom did not die.

**35**  When Marco Polo was a teenager, he left Venice with his father and uncle. Marco and the others traveled east, first by boat and then by land. They traveled all the way to China. For two decades they crisscrossed Asia. They spent a great deal of time visiting the court of the Chinese emperor. When Marco Polo returned, he told his story to a friend. His friend wrote the adventures in a book. The book was popular, but the stories sounded like a fantasy to most people.

**36**  Centuries ago, a group of Aztecs settled in a valley in central Mexico. They built one of their cities on an island. The swampy land was gradually dried to make more room. Land was also needed to produce food. Garden islands were created. Farmers fenced in part of the shallow lake bed and filled the area with soil. Willow trees were planted at the corners to help hold the soil in place. Many crops grew well on the rich soil of the new islands.

# Answer Key

Sometimes a word has overlapping chunks. For example, a vowel chunk may overlap with a Bossy *r* chunk (*heard*), or a consonant chunk may overlap with an ending (*really*). In the answer key, we have tried to remain consistent with the focus of each lesson. In lessons with multiple chunks, we marked vowel chunks before Bossy *r* chunks, but Bossy *r* chunks before consonant chunks.

If the student chooses a different chunking pattern than the one marked in the answer key, please do not consider it incorrect. Instead, take a moment to talk about the word and the overlap of chunks. You might ask the student which letter pattern he thinks would be most helpful for him to remember and let him mark that one. Remember that the goal is to create a visual memory for non-phonetic words.

**1:**

The Cave of Lascaux is one of the most famous caves in the world. One day four French teenagers were exploring. When the boys eased into a hidden cave, they were shocked! It was painted! Bison, deer, horses, cows, and bulls seemed to leap across the cave walls and ceilings. Some pictures showed people hunting animals. Thousands of years before, ancient people had painted these pictures. They had used minerals to make paints. They left behind a visual treasure.

**Word Count: 79     Vowel Chunks: 26**

**2:**

An airplane was flying over the German countryside near Goseck. The pilot saw a large circle in the wheat fields below. People had noticed similar circles before. Their purpose was a mystery. A group of young archeologists studied the Goseck Circle. They found four circles inside each other. One was a mound, and one was a ditch. Two of them were once marked with wooden fences. The gates in the fences lined up with the sun on certain days of the year. The circles may have helped people keep track of the seasons.

**Word Count: 93     Vowel Chunks: 26**

**3:**

Thousands of years ago, the Sumerians created a system of writing. It is called cuneiform. That's an odd name, but it actually makes sense. The name comes from the Latin word *cuneus*. It means *wedge*. The Sumerians used a wedge-shaped writing tool. They pressed this tool into damp clay tablets. Then the tablets were baked in the scorching sun. Writing was not the quick and easy process it is today. Some tablets lasted a long time. As a result, we know more about how people lived long ago.

**Word Count: 88**   <u>**Consonant Chunks:**</u> **27**

**4:**

The ancient Chinese had a secret. A person who shared the secret with others might be killed. This hidden knowledge started with a moth and a tree. Each moth laid eggs that produced silkworms. Each silkworm ate mulberry leaves. The worm produced a long, thin thread. The thread formed a cocoon. Women learned to harvest the cocoons at just the right time. They wove the threads into fine silk. For centuries, the Chinese guarded this secret. They traded their precious silk for other valuable products.

**Word Count: 85**   <u>**Consonant Chunks:**</u> **38**

**5:**

Ancient Egyptians believed it was important not to let a body decay after death. Rich people preserved bodies with great care. First, the brain was removed and discarded as worthless. Some organs were saved in jars. The heart was left in the body. To Egyptians, the heart was the center of reason. They washed the body and packed it in salts to dry. Weeks later, they wrapped it in cloth. Finally, they placed this mummy in a special coffin. The coffin was placed inside one or more larger coffins.

**Word Count: 89**   <u>**Vowel Chunks:**</u> **18**   <u>**Consonant Chunks:**</u> **26**

**6:**

"Time laughs at all things, but the pyramids laugh at time." That old saying seems true. Some pyramids have lasted so long they must be laughing! The Great Pyramid in Egypt was built thousands of years ago. Many other famous buildings are gone, but the Great Pyramid remains. It is massive. Its base covers 13 acres. It contains more than two million limestone and granite blocks. Some of the blocks weigh over two tons. It was built to house the pharaoh's body forever.

**Word Count: 83     Vowel Chunks: 21     Consonant Chunks: 21**

**7:**

The first rubber balls were made in Central America. People learned how to gather the sap of the rubber tree. They mixed the sap with the juice of the morning glory vine. When the rubber hardened, it could be used to make many things. Rubber balls were used for games. Many years later, explorers found some of these balls. However, the exact rules of the games are still a mystery.

**Word Count: 70     Bossy *r* Chunks: 21**

**8:**

The Greeks told stories about a war with Troy. After fighting for ten years, both sides were tired of the war. The Greeks made a clever plan. They built an enormous wooden horse. Their best warriors hid inside. The Greeks wheeled the horse to the gates of Troy and pretended to sail away. The people of Troy thought it was a gift. They wheeled the Trojan horse into their city. That was a major blunder! During the night, the Greek warriors slipped out of the Trojan horse and conquered Troy. The story of the Trojan War is still told today.

**Word Count: 100  Bossy *r* Chunks: 26**

**9:**

The Phoenicians lived near the sea. They built sturdy ships and sailed around the ancient world trading goods. Their ships carried olive oil and cedar wood to other ports. They sold purple dye and metalwork. As they sailed, they spread their alphabet. It used letters instead of pictures. The Greeks borrowed the alphabet and made some changes. The Romans changed it even more. A few letters in our alphabet still remind us of these older letters.

**Word Count: 76     Vowel Chunks: 24     Consonant Chunks: 26     Bossy *r* Chunks: 16**

**10:**

Ancient Greece was made up of city-states. People were fiercely loyal to their city-state. They were often at war with other city-states. Once a year they called a truce. Men gathered to compete in foot races. Every four years they met in Olympia for special events. These early Olympics grew to include sports such as boxing and wrestling. Later, events with horses were added. Women were allowed to compete in those events. The winners brought honor to their city-states.

**Word Count: 79     Vowel Chunks: 20     Consonant Chunks: 19     Bossy r Chunks: 14**

**11:**

A story from long ago tells about a king who married a woman from a far country. The woman became homesick for her own country. She missed the beauty of its green hills and mountains. The king's country was extremely hot, flat, and dry. The king decided to build his wife a garden as high as a mountain. Workers used bricks and stones to build it. They added terraces filled with soil, trees, and flowers. Storytellers called the king's gift the Hanging Gardens of Babylon. Ruins of gardens have been found in dry places.

**Word Count: 94     Tricky y Guy: 10**

**12:**

China was often attacked by tribes living to the north. One king built a stone wall even before China was an empire. The first Chinese emperor forced his people to build a wall. They mixed sand, gravel, and clay. This mixture was then packed into place. Wall building continued for many centuries. The walls usually didn't stop enemies. However, they were helpful in slowing down an army. The most famous wall is called the Great Wall of China. You can still see parts of this wall winding over hills and valleys.

**Word Count: 91     Endings: 15**

**13:**

Lighthouses have guided ships for centuries. One famous lighthouse was built at Alexandria, Egypt. It was about 400 feet high. Its purpose was to help ships find the harbor. What type of light shone in this lighthouse thousands of years ago? Fire! Light from this fire guided ships at night. Some people wrote that smoke could be seen during the day. Others believe that a huge mirror reflected the sun during the day. This lighthouse was a beacon to ships and a symbol of Alexandria.

**Word Count: 85    Silent Letters: 17**

**14:**

Thousands of years ago, the people of Athens tried something new. They didn't want to be ruled by one person or family. They created a new form of government. Citizens met often to discuss and debate. They made the laws. They also served in office. Only free men over 18 were citizens. Our word democracy comes from two Greek words. *Demos* means the common people of a country. *Kratos* means rule. In a democracy, the people rule.

**Word Count: 72    Vowel Chunks: 20    Consonant Chunks: 14    Bossy *r* Chunks: 9**
**Tricky *y* Guy: 5    Endings: 5    Silent Letters: 13**

(Note: The student may have chosen to mark the *-ly* in *family* instead of the *y*. The *ing* in *something* is part of the base word rather than an ending. Some students may identify the *tw* in *two* as a blend, in which case the *w* would not be marked as silent.)

**15:**

Chariot races were popular in ancient Greece. Horses burst from the starting gates. Men standing in chariots whipped their horses fiercely. The frenzy began! Fans cheered wildly for their favorite teams. Hooves thundered. Whips cracked. Dust rose thickly from the racetrack. At the turns, chariots often crashed into each other or into the side walls. Sometimes teams ran over the wrecked chariots. This kind of racing was a very risky sport!

**Word Count: 71    Vowel Chunks: 14    Consonant Chunks: 28    Bossy *r* Chunks: 18**
**Tricky *y* Guy: 3    Endings: 18    Silent Letters: 9**

**16:**

The Roman Empire grew in size and power over many centuries. It's no wonder! Its large army was a fighting machine. Soldiers were well trained and well organized. As they conquered more and more people, they acquired more and more land. The army built a system of roads throughout the vast empire. This helped soldiers travel quickly. They preferred to build straight roads. After all, marching around curves took more time! Roman roads were well built. Some of them lasted longer than the Empire.

**Word Count:** 84 **Vowel Chunks:** 21 **Consonant Chunks:** 24 **Bossy r Chunks:** 26
**Tricky y Guy:** 4 **Endings:** 11 **Silent Letters:** 16

**17:**

Two thousand years ago in the Philippines, some people faced a challenge. How could they farm the steep mountainsides where they lived? They planned and worked. They built walls of mud and stone. They created terraces along the sides of the mountains. A system of bamboo pipes was used to carry water down from the forest on top of the mountain. At first they grew a plant called taro. Later, each terrace became a rice paddy. With vision and hard work, they met the challenge of the mountain.

**Word Count:** 88 **Vowel Chunks:** 28 **Consonant Chunks:** 29 **Bossy r Chunks:** 13
**Tricky y Guy:** 3 **Endings:** 12 **Silent Letters:** 11

**18:**

Some of the world's treasures have been found by accident. One example is the Dead Sea Scrolls. A young man was tending his goats near the rugged shores of the Dead Sea. He noticed one goat was missing. As he searched the rocky terrain, he entered a cave. There he found clay jars with ancient scrolls inside. The scrolls were copies of many old books. Some of them were old copies of parts of the Hebrew Bible. Scholars believe these long-lost scrolls were hidden about 1900 years before they were found.

**Word Count:** 91 **Vowel Chunks:** 25 **Consonant Chunks:** 24 **Bossy r Chunks:** 14
**Tricky y Guy:** 3 **Endings:** 8 **Silent Letters:** 17

**19A–C:**

The Roman Empire had a civil war. There were three emperors in one year! Finally, an army general became emperor. He wanted to keep the people happy. That way they would not want to fight again. He ordered the Colosseum to be built. This building was a very large arena. It was built with concrete and stone. There were many arches for beauty and strength. The places where the emperor and nobles sat were decorated with marble. The ruins of the Colosseum still stand in the middle of Rome.

**Word Count: 89**   **Vowel Chunks: 15**   **Consonant Chunks: 25**   **Bossy r Chunks: 25**

**19D–E:**

The Roman Empire had a civil war. There were three emperors in one year! Finally, an army general became emperor. He wanted to keep the people happy. That way they would not want to fight again. He ordered the Colosseum to be built. This building was a very large arena. It was built with concrete and stone. There were many arches for beauty and strength. The places where the emperor and nobles sat were decorated with marble. The ruins of the Colosseum still stand in the middle of Rome.

**Word Count: 89**   **Tricky y Guy: 5**   **Endings: 8**   **Silent Letters: 17**

**20A–C:**

The Chinese were the first people to print books. Their language uses thousands of characters instead of a simple alphabet. For many years they carved each page into a wooden block. Later, each character was carved from clay. The characters were baked so they would harden. Next they were fastened onto iron plates. A page was printed from each plate. Thankfully the clay characters could be used over and over! The process was a challenge. Still, it was easier than copying books by hand.

**Word Count: 84**   **Vowel Chunks: 20**   **Consonant Chunks: 27**   **Bossy r Chunks: 21**

**20D–E:**

The Chinese were the first people to print books. Their language uses thousands of characters instead of a simple alphabet. For many years they carved each page into a wooden block. Later, each character was carved from clay. The characters were baked so they would harden. Next they were fastened onto iron plates. A page was printed from each plate. Thankfully the clay characters could be used over and over! The process was a challenge. Still, it was easier than copying books by hand.

**Word Count: 84**   **Tricky y Guy: 3**   **Endings: 11**   **Silent Letters: 13**

**21A–C:**

"Ready, aim, throw!" Before gunpowder and cannons were invented, armies used other machines to attack enemies from a distance. Some weapons stored tension in ropes. When the ropes were released, objects were hurled through the air. One weapon shot bolts. These were like arrows but were as big as spears. A different weapon hurled stones and fire over city walls. Later machines were built that could hurl stones as big as cars into castles.

**Word Count: 74**   **Vowel Chunks: 17**   **Consonant Chunks: 17**   **Bossy r Chunks: 20**

**21D–E:**

"Ready, aim, throw!" Before gunpowder and cannons were invented, armies used other machines to attack enemies from a distance. Some weapons stored tension in ropes. When the ropes were released, objects were hurled through the air. One weapon shot bolts. These were like arrows but were as big as spears. A different weapon hurled stones and fire over city walls. Later machines were built that could hurl stones as big as cars into castles.

**Word Count: 74**   **Tricky y Guy: 2**   **Endings: 15**   **Silent Letters: 15**

**22A–C:**

Timbuktu is a desert city in Africa. Camels carried salt from mines to the city. People traded the salt as well as gold and grain. One year the emperor traveled to Egypt. He spent a great deal of gold. People decided Timbuktu was very rich! Stories about the city also made it sound very mysterious. Scholars knew that the city had another treasure. It had libraries of handwritten books. People visited the city just to study these books.

**Word Count: 78**   **Vowel Chunks: 17**   **Consonant Chunks: 15**   **Bossy r Chunks: 12**

**22D–E:**

Timbuktu is a desert city in Africa. Camels carried salt from mines to the city. People traded the salt as well as gold and grain. One year the emperor traveled to Egypt. He spent a great deal of gold. People decided Timbuktu was very rich! Stories about the city also made it sound very mysterious. Scholars knew that the city had another treasure. It had libraries of handwritten books. People visited the city just to study these books.

**Word Count: 78**   **Tricky y Guy: 10**   **Endings: 8**   **Silent Letters: 7**

**23A–C:**

Minstrels entertained people by singing ballads and retelling stories. The legends of King Arthur were popular. One story tells about a sword stuck in a stone. Whoever pulled the sword from the stone was the rightful king. Many noblemen had already tried and failed. Young Arthur effortlessly removed the sword. Immediately he was crowned king. He reigned with the help of the Knights of the Round Table. King Arthur might not have been a real person, but the stories are still loved.

**Word Count: 82**   **Vowel Chunks: 15**   **Consonant Chunks: 28**   **Bossy r Chunks: 14**

**(Note: The *ing* in *king* is part of the word rather than an ending. The vowel chunk in *whoever* was not marked because *whoever* is a compound word made up of two separate words. If your student marked the oe chunk, discuss it but do not mark it wrong.)**

**23D–E:**

Minstrels entertained people by singing ballads and retelling stories. The legends of King Arthur were popular. One story tells about a sword stuck in a stone. Whoever pulled the sword from the stone was the rightful king. Many noblemen had already tried and failed. Young Arthur effortlessly removed the sword. Immediately he was crowned king. He reigned with the help of the Knights of the Round Table. King Arthur might not have been a real person, but the stories are still loved.

**Word Count: 82   Tricky y Guy: 4   Endings: 15   Silent Letters: 13**

**24A–C:**

Can you imagine trying to do math without the number zero? Some ancient people used columns to show place value. They wrote a special mark when a column was empty. It kept people from reading the wrong number. Then people in India began to use a symbol as a number that meant "none." Travelers brought this useful new number elsewhere. The idea of zero spread across the world. It opened the door to many new ideas in math.

**Word Count: 78   Vowel Chunks: 20   Consonant Chunks: 18   Bossy r Chunks: 10**

**24D–E:**

Can you imagine trying to do math without the number zero? Some ancient people used columns to show place value. They wrote a special mark when a column was empty. It kept people from reading the wrong number. Then people in India began to use a symbol as a number that meant "none." Travelers brought this useful new number elsewhere. The idea of zero spread across the world. It opened the door to many new ideas in math.

**Word Count: 78   Tricky y Guy: 4   Endings: 5   Silent Letters: 14**

**25:**

The Vikings lived by the North Sea. They became expert shipbuilders. For two centuries, they used their longships to raid the lands around them. The design of the ships made them ideal for the job. They could be used in very shallow water, so the rivers soon became highways to places far from the coastline. Very thin hulls made the ships lightweight and easy to maneuver. A crew of warriors used oars to propel the ship. Sometimes a sail was used as well. Some of the Vikings also made their homes in the lands they had raided.

**Word Count:** 97   **Vowel Chunks:** 25   **Consonant Chunks:** 35   **Bossy *r* Chunks:** 14

**Tricky *y* Guy:** 4   **Endings:** 9   **Silent Letters:** 10

(Note: The *ing* in *Vikings* is part of the word rather than an ending. However, do not consider it wrong if your student marked it.)

**26:**

When Charlemagne became king, life was difficult. People used most of their energy to grow food and keep safe from enemies. The king thought that books and learning were important. He created places where books could be copied and saved. He started schools where people could learn to read and write. He even tried to learn to read and write for himself. The schools also taught other subjects such as arithmetic and astronomy. Some of the king's ideas about education are still popular today.

**Word Count:** 84   **Vowel Chunks:** 27   **Consonant Chunks:** 21   **Bossy *r* Chunks:** 12

**Tricky *y* Guy:** 2   **Endings:** 6   **Silent Letters:** 16

**27:**

Imagine being on the scene when gunpowder was first discovered. According to old reports, some Chinese men were mixing different substances. They were trying to create a mixture that would prolong life. As they heated their mixture, it began to burn. Suddenly there was an explosion. What a shock! The men were caught off guard. Their hands and faces were badly burned. The place where they were working burned to the ground. It probably didn't take them long to realize their discovery would never prolong life.

**Word Count:** 86   **Vowel Chunks:** 16   **Consonant Chunks:** 24   **Bossy *r* Chunks:** 21

**Tricky *y* Guy:** 2   **Endings:** 14   **Silent Letters:** 22

(Note: Your student may have marked the *ei* vowel chunk in *being* instead of the ending. Also, some students may hear the *sc* in *scene* as a blend, so they would not mark the *c* as silent.)

**28:**

Most buildings are made from many pieces. Can you imagine a building made from just one block of stone? If you travel to Lalibela in Ethiopia, you will see some very old churches. They are carved out of solid rock. Some of them were hewn into the side of a mountain. Others were made by cutting straight down into the rock from the top of a hill. First the outside of the building was cut from the rock. Then the inside was hollowed out. Windows and decorations were also carved. The buildings are about 900 years old. They are still used today.

**Word Count: 102  Vowel Chunks: 27  Consonant Chunks: 26  Bossy r Chunks: 14
Tricky y Guy: 3  Endings: 11  Silent Letters: 18**

**29:**

During the Middle Ages, knights kept improving their armor. Eventually, they went into battle dressed from head to toe in heavy metal suits. Even their horses were covered in metal armor. This caused a problem. On the battlefield all the knights looked similar. Who was an ally? Who was an enemy? It was hard to tell the difference! Each family designed a unique coat of arms. The knights of that family painted this coat of arms on their armor. A father passed the family coat of arms down to his sons. The problem was solved!

**Word Count: 95  Vowel Chunks: 18  Consonant Chunks: 34  Bossy r Chunks: 17
Tricky y Guy: 2  Endings: 17  Silent Letters: 6**

**(Note: For *eventually* and *ally*, your student may have chosen to mark the *ll* as a consonant chunk and the *y* as Tricky y Guy.)**

**30:**

Does the thought of leeches make you shudder? Leeches are a kind of worm that feeds on blood from other animals. For centuries, physicians believed that some diseases were caused by having too much blood. They often used leeches as a remedy. The leeches attached themselves to a patient's skin. Then they drew blood out of the veins. Leeches produce a substance that prevents blood from clotting. As a result, the blood kept flowing. The leeches kept filling up with blood until they could not hold any more.

**Word Count: 88  Vowel Chunks: 31  Consonant Chunks: 31  Bossy r Chunks: 8
Tricky y Guy: 4  Endings: 16  Silent Letters: 9**

**31:**

Have you ever heard of Robin Hood? Stories say that he was an outlaw who stole from the rich to help the poor. Robin Hood may only be a legend, but the type of bow he used in the stories was real. The Welsh longbow was a powerful weapon. Drawing the bowstring required a lot of strength. Men needed to practice a long time before they could shoot quickly and accurately. King Edward the Third wanted skilled English archers. He said that every man had to practice with his longbow on Sundays and holidays.

**Word Count:** 94  **Vowel Chunks:** 26  **Consonant Chunks:** 24  **Bossy _r_ Chunks:** 11
**Tricky _y_ Guy:** 2  **Endings:** 10  **Silent Letters:** 9

**32:**

Why is the Leaning Tower of Pisa so famous? It seems to defy gravity. The building has been leaning for over 800 years. The foundation was not built deeply enough. The soil under it settled unevenly. Years ago people stopped ringing the bells in the tower. Scientists thought the vibrations would make the tower fall. Recent work strengthened the tower while keeping the famous lean. Now the bells are rung again. Visitors can climb nearly 300 steps to the top.

**Word Count:** 80  **Vowel Chunks:** 29  **Consonant Chunks:** 23  **Bossy _r_ Chunks:** 9
**Tricky _y_ Guy:** 3  **Endings:** 11  **Silent Letters:** 7

**33:**

Different people have recorded information in different ways. Some etched pictures. Some groups of people drew symbols. Some used characters or alphabets to write words. The Incas had a unique system for recording numbers. They tied knots on strings. Different colored strings were attached to a base to keep them organized. Three different types of knots stood for ones, tens, and hundreds. The knotted strings were called quipus. They were used to keep track of data such as work done and taxes paid. Many things about the quipus are still a mystery.

**Word Count:** 92  **Vowel Chunks:** 15  **Consonant Chunks:** 29  **Bossy _r_ Chunks:** 23
**Tricky _y_ Guy:** 6  **Endings:** 14  **Silent Letters:** 14

**34:**

King John thought that kings were above the law. He taxed the English people heavily. He seized any land that he wanted. He arrested people who disagreed with him. In short, he did whatever he felt like doing. Powerful noblemen grew angry about having a tyrant for their king. Finally they acted. They forced the king to accept the Magna Carta, or Great Charter. This document guaranteed certain rights to free men. King John did not keep the agreement, but the idea of freedom did not die.

**Word Count:** 87    **Vowel Chunks:** 23    **Consonant Chunks:** 21    **Bossy r Chunks:** 12

**Tricky y Guy:** 3    **Endings:** 11    **Silent Letters:** 8

**35:**

When Marco Polo was a teenager, he left Venice with his father and uncle. Marco and the others traveled east, first by boat and then by land. They traveled all the way to China. For two decades they crisscrossed Asia. They spent a great deal of time visiting the court of the Chinese emperor. When Marco Polo returned, he told his story to a friend. His friend wrote the adventures in a book. The book was popular, but the stories sounded like a fantasy to most people.

**Word Count:** 87    **Vowel Chunks:** 18    **Consonant Chunks:** 22    **Bossy r Chunks:** 15

**Tricky y Guy:** 4    **Endings:** 8    **Silent Letters:** 8

**36:**

Centuries ago, a group of Aztecs settled in a valley in central Mexico. They built one of their cities on an island. The swampy land was gradually dried to make more room. Land was also needed to produce food. Garden islands were created. Farmers fenced in part of the shallow lake bed and filled the area with soil. Willow trees were planted at the corners to help hold the soil in place. Many crops grew well on the rich soil of the new islands.

**Word Count:** 84    **Vowel Chunks:** 22    **Consonant Chunks:** 18    **Bossy r Chunks:** 11

**Tricky y Guy:** 2    **Endings:** 7    **Silent Letters:** 11

# Glossary

*Adjective* – a word that describes or modifies a noun

*Adverb* – a word that describes or modifies a verb, adjective, or another adverb

*Affix* – a letter or group of letters added to the beginning or end of a word. It may indicate a tense or a plural, or it may completely change the meaning of the base word. *Prefixes* and *suffixes* are two kinds of affixes.

*Base word* – a word that has meaning by itself. The meaning of a base word may be changed or expanded by adding letters to the beginning or end of the word.

*Blend* – two or more consonants that appear together but keep their distinct sounds. Words like *flag*, *stop*, and *stream* begin with blends, and the word *fast* ends with a blend. A blend is different from a consonant chunk because all the sounds of the consonants are heard.

*Bossy r* – a letter pattern in which a vowel is followed by an *r* that controls ("bosses") the vowel by changing its sound

*Chunk* – a particular letter pattern that occurs frequently in English and which may not have a predictable sound

*Chunking* – the process of finding and marking all the designated letter patterns in a particular passage

*Consonant* – any letter of the alphabet that is not a vowel. The consonants are *b, c, d, f, g, h, j, k, l, m, n, p, q, r, s, t, v, w, x, y*, and *z*.

*Compound word* – a word made by combining two other words. Compound words maybe written as one word, two words, or with a hyphen.

*Consonant chunks* – a combination of two or more consonants that usually make a single sound. Consonant chunks may also be silent.

*Copywork* – words or sentences provided for a student to copy

*Decode* – use letter-to-sound correspondance to read a word in print

*Dictation* – the process of reading a sentence or passage aloud and having the student write it without looking at the passage

*Encode* – create a word from individual sounds

*Etymology* – the study of the history of words

*Noun* – a word that names a person, place, thing, or idea

*Phonemic awareness* – the ability to distinguish the individual sounds that make up spoken words

*Phonics* – the study of the sounds usually indicated by letters and combinations of letters in a particular language

*Plural* – the form of a noun that indicates more than one person, place, thing, or idea

*Prefix* – a letter or group of letters added to the beginning of a word to alter the meaning of the word

*Preliterate* – the developmental stage of spelling at which children begin to become familiar with the idea of written language

*Rhyming words* – two or more words that have the same ending sounds. They may or may not have the same spelling patterns.

*Root* – a word or part of a word that carries a specific meaning. A word root can help with spelling by showing relationships between words that seem to be unrelated to each other.

*Silent letter* – a letter that is included when spelling a word but has no sound when the word is pronounced

**Suffix** – a letter or group of letters added to the end of a word to alter the meaning of the word. It may indicate tense or plural, or completely change the meaning of the base word.

**Syllable** – a word or part of a word pronounced as a single unit. It consists of one vowel sound and often the consonant sounds that cluster around it.

**Tense** – the form of a verb that tells when the action occurred

**Tricky y Guy** – a *y* in the middle or at the end of a word that is sounded as a vowel instead of as a consonant

**Verb** – a word that expresses action or a state of being

**Vowel** – one of the letters *a, e, i, o,* and *u.* Sometimes *y* and *w* also act as vowels. Every word in the English language has at least one vowel sound.

**Vowel chunks** – a combination of two or more vowels. A vowel chunk usually has a single sound.

# Bibliography

This curriculum is based on years of research into how children learn to read and spell. Here are some of the resources that were used in the development of this program.

Berk, L. E., & Winsler, A. (1995). *Scaffolding children's learning: Vygotsky and early childhood education.* Washington, DC: National Association for the Education of Young Children.

Clay, M. M. (1991). *Becoming literate: The construction of inner control.* Portsmouth, NH: Heinemann.

Clay, M. M. (2010). *What changes in writing can I see?* Portsmouth, NH: Heinemann.

Cook, D. L. (1992). *When your child struggles: The myths of 20/20 vision: What every parent needs to know.* Atlanta, GA: Invision Press.

Cunningham, P. M. (2012). *Phonics they use: Words for reading and writing* (6th ed.). New York, NY: Pearson.

Flanigan, K., Hayes, L., Templeton, S., Bear, D. R., Invernizzi, M. R., & Johnston, F. (2011). *Words their way with struggling readers: Word study for reading, vocabulary, and spelling instruction, grades 4–12.* Boston, MA: Allyn & Bacon.

Fountas, I. C., & Pinnell, G. S. (Eds). (1999). *Voices on word matters: Learning about phonics and spelling in the literacy classroom.* Portsmouth, NH: Heinemann.

Ganske, K. (2008). *Mindful of words: Spelling and vocabulary explorations 4–8 (Solving problems in teaching of literacy).* New York, NY: Guilford Press.

Heilman, A. W. (1968). *Phonics in proper perspective.* (2nd ed.). Columbus, OH: Charles E. Merrill Publishing Company.

Henderson, E. H. (1990). *Teaching spelling* (2nd ed.). Boston, MA: Houghton Mifflin.

Levine, M. (2000). *Educational care: A system for understanding and helping children with learning differences at home and in school* (2nd ed.). Cambridge, MA: Educators Publishing Service.

Lyons, C. A. (2003). *Teaching struggling readers: How to use brain-based research to maximize learning.* Portsmouth, NH: Heinemann.

McCarrier, A., Pinnell, G. S., & Fountas, I. C. (2000). *Interactive writing: How language and literacy come together, K–2.* Portsmouth, NH: Heinemann.

Pinnell, G. S., & Fountas, I. C. (1998). *Word matters: Teaching phonics and spelling in the reading/writing classroom.* Portsmouth, NH: Heinemann.

Read, C. (1971). Pre-school children's knowledge of English phonology. *Harvard Educational Review,* 41(1), 150–179.

Sprenger, M. (1999). *Learning and memory: The brain in action.* Alexandria, VA: Association for Supervision and Curriculum Development.

Wood, D. (1988). *How children think and learn: The social contexts of cognitive development.* Cambridge, MA: Blackwell Publishers.

Zutell, J. (1998). Word sorting: A developmental spelling approach to word study for delayed readers. *Reading and Writing Quarterly,* 14(2), 219–238.

# Index of Topics